CYBORGIA

CYBORGIA

POEMS BY SUSAN SLAVIERO

MAYAPPLE PRESS 2010

Published by   MAYAPPLE PRESS
                408 N. Lincoln St.
                Bay City, MI 48708
                www.mayapplepress.com

ISBN 978-0932412-90-4

ACKNOWLEDGMENTS

Artifice Magazine: "Pandora's Robot" "Phenomena of Probability"; *Blood Pudding Press / Spider Vein Impasto*: "Agalmatophilia" "Robosexual" "Anatomy of the Grotesque" "Taxonomy: Cyborg M/Others"; *Ditch*: "Our Lady of X-Ray Vision" "Sleepwalker" "Zeroes & Ones"; *Eclectica*: "Our Lady of Machinery" "The Mechanician" "A Modern Synthesis"; *Dante's Heart*: "Little Red and the Robot Wolf" "Postmodern Werewolves"; *Fickle Muses*: "Bluebeard's Clockwork Bride" "Briar Rose, in Cryostasis"; *Kaliedotrope*: "If Snow White Were a Cyborg"; *Word For / Word*: "Postcorporeal" "Femmes Fatales Digitales" "Manifesto for Ghosts"; *Spooky Boyfriend*: "Origin Story"; *Sein Und Werden*: "VirtualGirl III: A Space Opera"; *A Trunk of Delirium / Le Pink Elephant Press*: "Evolution of the Villain Protagonist" "Mechanized Bride"

Special thanks go to Simone Muench, for believing I had what it takes to write a book, and to Melissa Culbertson, for telling me this collection of poems was *that* book. Thank you to Marissa Frattini for her wonderful photography skills and for always knowing how to create art that supports the text. Additional gratitude to my husband Mike, for watching science fiction movies with me even though spaceships make him feel sleepy. Finally, thank you to Judith Kerman and the staff of Mayapple Press for making beautiful books, including this one.

Cover photos courtesy of iStockphoto.com. Cover designed by Marissa Frattini and Judith Kerman. Book designed and typeset by Amee Schmidt with cover titles in Weltron Urban, poem titles in Centaur and text in Californian FB. Author photo courtesy of Marissa Frattini.

CONTENTS

The Red Queen Hypothesis

明胶

Celluloid Marionettes

Boolean Fairy Tales

Ontology of the Virtual Body

"I would rather be a cyborg than a goddess."

—Donna Haraway

"Now here, you see, it takes all the running
you can do to keep in the same place."

—Lewis Carroll

THE RED QUEEN HYPOTHESIS

Postcorporeal

Look, changeling. (調包)
No one would suspect

the monsterskin rustling
beneath your latex fleshtones.
氣泡 膚色

The hiss of air
in your helmet when you mimic

抽筋
the tic in a woman's eye.
流氓/Rogue genes

are not the ash in your mechanical boots,
the schizophrenic scattering of light
精神分裂

from the side you can't touch.
Accidental kleptomaniac, 盗窃者

your magnetic fingers
wicked at the pulse of a man's throat.

Now, the signal is set to vibrate.
You are outmoded anatomy. 骨骼，解剖

Look, prototype. 核型 蓝图
You are destined to survive

on hostile planets.
This ruin should be easy

as a saltwater catastrophe,
as red fruit crushed against a woman's lips.

发情
Your rutting mechanism.
Your surface etching. 不露 感情，刻记

Naked, you are all *hello, holograph.* 親筆写
What prophetess said *swallow?*
女预言家

::7::

Phenomena of Probability

Theoretically, there's a way to create a ribcage from guitar strings, to
fashion jawbones from vintage bracelets. It so happens that a female
frame is best woven from titanium knitting needles, peppermint hips,
the ends of French cigarettes. The dog might notice she isn't real, but
no one else can tell the difference. You'll find she is content

to collect matchsticks for weeks on end. At home she is a semicolon,
a subtle separation between your horsefly hands and the Japanese
lanterns on the ceiling. She wears a divining rod around her neck
that only finds tangerines in dry weather. You reach for a girl in the
kitchen, find only robot parts

because she is bathing in the porcelain sink. The room smells of salt-
water and seashells even though you live in Indiana. You believe the
Virgin Mary might appear in a partially-melted chocolate bar because
if a convincing tongue can be constructed of raw velvet then anything
is possible. You mark her back

with indelible ink. *Waitful*, you write, *spoonlike*. When guests arrive,
they comment on how green your mornings, how thumblike your
lovely wife. How lyrical. How much like a warm bun. She plays the
viola while making supper. Someday, she will be a box of fragments
cluttering your attic. Someday, you will decide you prefer mermaids.

The Mechanician

knows that a woman without veins has no use
for a tourniquet. That she takes calcium pills
hoping to grow bones. He fashions her a solenoid

spine, electromagnetic thumbs, pulleys at her hips
and shoulders. She is milk and smoke, a dash
of candlepower, her wire antennae clacking

like ice cubes in a tumbler of gin. He labels her
vixen/mistress/bitch. Imagines her in a shirtwaist
and pearls watching television talk shows, cooking

three-course meals in the microwave. She is fond
of fish. Her hair, braided filaments shimmering
under the solar lights. A halotrope. A phantasmagoria.

She loves it when he speaks to her in binary code,
turns her on with tight little strokes of her power
switch. She was born twice from black water

he says. Once, she was feral. Once, she was ruins.

A Modern Synthesis 綜合

The way she looks, you'd think
zippers do not exist. Only latch-hooks

焊点

and buttons. No tight welds at her waistline,
or tiny speakers where her lips should be.

In the right kind of shadow, she could be
drinking milk. You might try and open her up

with a screwdriver, looking for rainwater
and wristwatches, perhaps a password

解码

to decrypt those fetal markings on the soles
of her feet, the tattoos of clockwork eyes

齿叉

and fork tines, silver keyholes that collect
in the hollows of her metallic limbs.

相和地制作，卵石.

She is the cobbled remains of old
calendars—corsets and prisms, a hunger 欲望

胸罩衣   苹果林

for apples. A mythology swallowed
with aspirin and coffee. The taste

of salt. You were there. Something female
was alive. Something shivered in the icebox.

Robosexual

The unwritten eggs beneath her veil,
aluminum legbones, a locust husk,
the embroidery of her threaded tongue.
I allow for flux, fissure,
for saints kneeling on upturned spoons.
This scene is about design.

Later, under girl-cheek moons,
she drizzles spittle on a man's abdomen.
The poppies on her helmet disguise
starlike dents, a row of rivets. Wake up
and bend in unexpected ways.
A needle is warmed in the glimmer
of a kitchen match. You might be lulled
by the cut of her jaw, the unwinding
of her limbs. You might be hooked
on rubber dolls. You might be licking
your own reflection.

Femmes Fatales Digitales

轮廓

The contours of knees turned

模拟 性交   氨基酸   灵魂

inwards. Teledildonics + folklore + amino acids. Doppelganger

pop-art, nonhuman [?]   projective fantasies

of men wearing girls' bodies, tethered 系链

at the root, body = zero   prostheses, a little cellular 细胞

[copy] born under

    the sign of X.

凹曲 凸面

Concave, convex. Urban

        names

           that don't figure

in your scissor-blade psychoanalysis. 心理分析

We are wearing this apparatus. 装置·组织

Cold-clones. Flatscreen

    mystics. 神秘

(We promise you this is [hyper]reality.)

    [   ] now in uncanny matrices. 矩阵

    神秘

Agalmatophilia

This surgeon-sealed Kore, holding thistles in her mauled hands.

> Between the manga pages, a Japanese gynoid
> holds a gun. Bleeds oil into mailboxes. Says
> "Force, time, acceleration." She'll brew
> green tea for ghosts, sip sake from a doll's
> porcelain brainpan.

Venus de Milo or jerky machinery? This Madonna
is under construction. Check the diagram, the smoky
cleft between her thighs.

> Over time, the dream sequence dissolves
> into oxygen and heat, the hum of wires
> around a synthetic patella.

She imagines herself in contraceptive places—the lost cities
of Nebraska. She sees you as architecture, as blue libido.

Pandora's Robot

opened the brass plate over her sternum

and let out language.

Let out codes

like *apocalypse, alchemy, calculus.*

((Still, there is a plum fluttering in her ribcage,

a galaxy furled in her wire rigging.))

Mechanics call her

:: bonethief :: :: trickster :: :: minx ::

[?] How many milkdrowned homunculi

have called her [MOTHER] [?]

[?] If this transmission is intercepted

{slipstopped box}

is she dismantled, rebuilt

like chaos

whirring backwards

into singularity [?]

A collapsing husk, 外壳 ·

        equator of bone.

Metal. Lung.   Respiration // Expiration

        ((Thrum))

What pinprick? 针刺

What prick?

Parthenogenesis

Your body pares away these
budding whiptail virgins

                         that evolve into red queens
                         if you feed them enough hellebore.

Seeded and blood-blistered.
These offspring are variations

                         on your cutting-edge
                         mechanism, a maternal response

to an ever-changing bed.
They are more than greening

                         myth, reedy little bones
                         that solidify in sunlight.

They are carnivorous lineage.
When they say *Off With Her*

                         Head, they mean you.
                         You figure they are fire signs

so that's to be expected.
Your daughters are live-bearing

                         and asymmetrical. Once you
                         are gone, they will produce

only drones. They are hungry,
so you offer them a transfusion

                         of your pale cellulose
                         a lick of flame

from your rounded heart.
They smoke cigarettes

> while you sleep, learning
> to resist the pull of your blue

vessels, the undertow
of your splitting shell.

Now, a list of ingredients for the post-human ((cyborg)) body

butterfly throat :: diecast bronze :: dexterous clockwork arms
pouring libations of vodka :: an air-driven polymer muscle ::
"robosexuality" :: limblike specter :: Galatea :: Vulcan :: collapsing
swarm :: an orange in the snow :: failure to metaphor :: fire sensors ::
technophilia as applied to toothbrushes :: doves and scars :: alliteration
and sequins :: a cultured flask of mitochondria :: two mechanized
hearts :: riboflavin :: a plague of blackberries 核黄素

Gynoid Eve

I strip down to the visibly mechanical when the genesis of a chromium
rib pushes against the meat beneath my silicon skin. When I sleep,
I synthesize cherries into bullets, tobacco leaves into wristblades.
    Don't ask me how I do it.

I am built to withstand sulfur volcanoes, ammonium air. They say I am
part daemon / part robot, reanimated with supple metallic limbs
and acid spit. I can dissolve your wetware with a French kiss, a well
      executed lick across your back. Here, the oceans burn

like a fictional dystopia. There is no molecular solution. Cyberdogs
chew at the walls of our Eden, tasting copper and keratin, sticking
paws into stacks of pilfered spines, wagging cybernetic tails.
    I name them after human teeth:

Bicuspid, Molar, Incisor. I am partially organic. I could hunt,
but I prefer to list the names of amorphous metals on the tops
of my thighs. I cannot shake the sense of vertigo I feel
      when Adam shows me his internal weapons.

He has a crossbow in his chest, air-cannons in his forearms. We are built
to withstand this primitive gutting, to swallow our conscience
at the sight of ruptured hide. No matter what he brings home for dinner
      it tastes like apples and albumen.

Because sometimes she's more fishflesh than sexbot.
Because an empty body is not subject to the laws

of gravity. Or addiction. She stuttered upon ignition,
fell mute. Her doll-pupils blank and blown.

Because this version is more chimerical than intended.
The systematic removal of her organs reveals rust,

bovine pathology, serpentine viscera. This model
brings to mind words like *lesion, trauma.*

Because there is a fetus in her thorax,
and proper placement is essential to evolution.

Because a wrench is labeled *love-device.*

分类空 （分类学）

[Gynoid Reproductive Mechanism]

人工刻印　产科学　注射器　胚胎

Take an artifact as obstetric: a syringe, an embryo, a birth machine
designed to uncouple alien knots, to dilute biological materials with
无菌 sterile fluid. This is the rhetoric of self-insemination on the kitchen
table. Of a femme fatale swallowing six bones. Imagine the fission of
purple screams, wicked pincers at her prosthetic breast.

女人在哪里？　土地耶　假乳头

胎儿胎盘 *[Fetoplacental Unit]*。

母系的　孵化的

Entire matrilineal lines are flattened under the weight of spawned
objects. Occult terms for texture, murder. Anomalies of stillbirth and
spiderbabies with jointed mechanical legs. Eugenic singularity. An
焰放 ethereal midwife. A dark red mass in a metal pan.

接生婆.

[Pathogen] 病原体

哺乳　光轮

Seed-sown, this is the riddle of lactation. A nimbus of heat around
a vulva. Something parasitic. A dash of chora, a talent for mimesis. 模仿
女阴
Something sharp-clawed and beautifully constructed. Cells ruptured
by organelles evolving tentacles while she sleeps.

细胞器.　触须

Anatomy of the Grotesque

One cannot separate *flesh* from *burn*—
this thing we call woman wilts under your tongue.
A steel-toothed gear as *mouth concept*,

as *dirty allegory*. Some designs triangulate
around well-dressed meat, porcelain gypsies,
undressed stomachs and celebrity cameos

in sci-fi flicks with nonlinear narratives
and Dutch angles; oddly-lit and dim-green
with magnetic gloom clouds and sizzling guns.

Pink-shellacked bodies, transparent segments
revealing miniature sparrow-lungs, flowering
kidneys wired to their lower ribs. They might

be spherical, pregnant with electric-blue babies
and superfluous hands wriggling in gel the color
of bloodless plasma. This is a beautiful horror.

Mechanized Bride

The phenomenon is sex-by-proxy, 代理人
the (re)insertion of rogue text.
I am (hyper)textual, an alien

automaton (dis)arranged by median 中央
nerve fibers. You jacked in
to my dollslot, called me a slick witch.

Your chimerical heroin(e).
We are (re)configuring this utopia
where every phantasm is a cyborg

butterfly. What skull-drugs figure
in your iridium correlations?
I am (self-)aware, a new version

of noir slut to your outlaw player.
I add horror to your hypothesis. 假設

CELLULOID MARIONETTES

Cyborg Cowgirl

影像

Perfect simulacrum. I am organs & nerves,
an icon automated by light waves,
electrical charges & discharges. A waxwork

周圍

cyberdoll. Schematic of the body-blank.
仿效 Villainess rippling in witchfire, a mosaic 用格仔做的畫
of human eyes on my hollowed-out chassis. 底盤

My gunslinger arms rolling loose & inhuman.
A woman casting analog 摸似 codes in the direction
of the old west. A turn-key metaphor

for collage, piecework. I might vanquish 征服
a two-headed alien with my samurai sword.
My every programmed expression a pleasure

散发

mask, an emanation of O. I'll say *ocotillo*, *opium*.
Manipulate my lips into the shape of round berries.
Outline my sexaroid features in obsidian ink.

黑曜石

Evolution of the Villain Protagonist

Even automata have vertigo in funneled spaces.
We know this happens when everything bleeds

sepia, when Conestoga wagons morph into space-
ships and not all the dance hall girls are buxom

and befeathered. Someone always shoots the dog
in the most climactic scene. Once you activate

the killswitch, the rest is merely clockwork
devoid of absolute value, of interlocking tropes

that are simultaneously hard-boiled and cool-
handed. This double-fisted firing mimics

intoxication, animatronic bones. The man
in the black longcoat shifts netward, towards

resurrection, the *deus ex machina* / dark synthesis.

Why We Never Call It Devolution

The sometimes-swallowing of a disguise.
One cybergirl does not make a swarm 蜂群.

intellect, or even an evolutionary schema. 图解
The boy with the metallic endoskeleton 内骨骼,

伴随的衍生
might be a spinoff, or just a flicker
in the protagonist's compound retinae. 视网膜

男画
She might interface with a pinecone 松果
or a lotus, because the boy is all shells

雪柏
and implants. Whatever he is, she is
splitting his mechanical aspect from

摆弄
skinjobs and data-jacks. In this story,
he is reborn until he bleeds white.

The girl will witness something cellular
and kinetic, like replication. Maybe
动力学   复制

复活
she is a villain who resurrects an army
using echolocation and replaceable parts.
回声定位

This is something you might see
in a textbook, or the opening crawl 爬行.

解说者声音
of a film where the voiceover says,
This is symbiotic. This is how we gravitate. 引力

Portmanteau

The girlborg is a mimic, the modification of suppleskin, guns akimbo,
in this fullmetal ghostopia. A town where sarsaparilla arrives in a sug-
arglass, and a crushed moth might be recycled as an eyelid if you can
manufacture the right combination of chemicals and prefixes. A long-
coat is nothing like a shotglass, but they both exist in the same saloon.
She is just as much an operation as a Molotov cocktail. She could
spurkick your eyes to slitblack, the saved memory of bloodshade on
a noonshot street, if only you weren't wearing this antigravity device,
or morphing into a black hat without an antagonist. Later, you will
unpack your holster and find a smokestick that isn't a revolver, isn't
even a trigger.

Origin Story

There can't be a game without a gun. Where we start,
a leitmotif of the digital dead, resurrection myths
or a virus hidden in a Trojan tinderbox. All
humanoid shapes are suspect. Seamless bodies,
hand-cranked and barely clad in husks of alloy,
discordant tones. A nun might ask the coordinates
for the first-ever immaculate birth on screen.
Dropping the womb entirely. We suffer amnesia
of the body, believe anything can emerge
from a stoma. A dragon. Artichoke hearts.
A prophet that looks like a hologram but isn't.

Sleepwalker

Bloodformed letters on her collar
or siphoned ink, a red scent.

When she hallucinates, it's the real thing—
motel-drifters, metalwomen smoking

long cigarettes in poolhalls with fermented
sailors. They are infosick, huffing

skulldust and mouthwash vapors.
The underpinnings of psychotic visions.

Nanobrain, hydraulic spine. The wheeze
of gears under fluorescent lights—

these lead ladies are tradpezoids, furrowed
flesh. The deadfall of microparticles

caught on film. Only the photo
is void. Burned at the margins.

A woman on the freeway steers
with an automated hook-hand.

She smiles, silver-fanged,
a twist of licorice in her lips.

She is the somnambulist's symptom X.

Radioactive mind-music—
                 andante, allegro.

Triptych with Female Cyborg

Surveillance (I)

Don't you know the roots of lead
in the blood, of cigarettes & stickpins,
of dead scenes embedded in a hairline
fracture, divided by tendons & ligaments,
scabgrass in the steel sidewalks. I read her
feline intent in the arch of an eyebrow,
her penny neckline.

Jezebel (II)

See her as cups & hammers, a tot
of ice-cold gin. An ovary is smashed
beneath her kittenheel, leaking barbiturates
into oilslicks. Note the panic marks
on her throat, the tangents beneath
her fingernails. These dogs are fiction.
These dogs are hysteric. What eight-
ball embryo fits into the framework of her
spirals & lines, her bionic knifeboot?

Keloid Formation (III)

There is red paint in her teeth
to simulate the stain of pomegranate.
This is the replica of a woman's cheek,
her carotid pulse. These crisscross scars
are really welded cracks in her carapace,
the stain of ether. Inside a green bottle
is the breath that simulates sleep,
the screen's refractive opiate
that sees you scratching.

VirtualGirl III: A Space Opera

*

Once upon a time a brain in a belljar was expanding. A universe
we killed because we had to. Feedback. Random patterns
of pixels and bones. This is *quintessence*. This *is*.

*

Doll blueprints. Shadowing jackals only to discover
they are simulacra. Chisel :: hammer :: fork :: a screendeath
for the antihero. A new character is introduced. Try to pay attention.

*

Metalflesh, unknitting at the joints. Links and bonds.
This connection winking out in vestigial stages. GRIDlock.
HATchet WOUnd. They call her *entity*, but she is porous, fluid.

*

She seeps yellow liquid, analogous to blood. Spasm.
Writhe. Identify her alienskin by posture, gesture.
The repulsion one feels when choking on a bolt.

*

[REMOTE VIEW] *Pulse, glow. The chill*
of negative space. Panopticon. Three fevered
hearts swarming in a blue-lit aquarium.

Spontaneous Visual Impressions
from an Ocular Implant

i. A great black bird with mechanical wings. In the distance, plumes of reddish smoke.

ii. A post-apocalyptic landscape, smoldering rubble. A woman with blue hands is holding a sheaf of wheat.

iii. A man with golden skin steps out into the moonlight. Coral snakes wind themselves around his arms and legs.

iv. The ocean is teeming with cybernetic sharks. Their knifelike dorsal fins protrude from a bed of rolling white foam.

v. There is now a cyborg with bare metallic breasts. She appears to be sleeping as orange flames encircle her.

vi. Singed bodies on a slag-heap.

vii. A telepathic being with greenish skin smokes a cigarette.

viii. A broadsword. Viscous fluids oozing from a severed arm.

ix. A woman lights a candlestub, affixes it to the center of an unbodied palm. When she plants the hand in the earth, it transforms into a robotic baby whose cries resemble whalesong.

Bride of Frankenstein 2.0

I wake in a state of clitoral arousal.
I hear the cadence of my own dissection.
Dark, festering segments replaced
with long curves of choreographed glass.
The clink-tink of a wrench in my

⟨digitized⟩

pelvis. What magic? An after/image of generativity.
I am the (dys)recognition of a two-sexed
system. My metalhood is evolution.
See, Zombie? You've always wanted a terminal
virgin, hinged in all the hot places. This flat
affect is characteristic of my vampire

⟨species⟩

I will not burn, even at blue temperatures.
I'll be your nickel marionette, a (fac)simile,
the spread of silver between your legs,
casting reflections of coitus on the ceiling.
I am loops and angles, a slight copper
taint on your tongue—

⟨inorganic⟩

oils and welded plates. Now available
in either decorative brass or stainless

⟨steel⟩

Consider the Dangers of Reconstructing
Your Wife As a Cyborg

1.
If you ask, I will explain the paradox of a virus that infects only metal.
I am not your celluloid marionette. Not marriage material, or hulled
fruit. You think I am cruel as the moon, but really, I am the ghost of
your formulations: aluminum and simmered bones. But I remember
skin and strawberries, the need for bandages, the scent of laundry
soap and baking powder on Saturdays. I'm not saying that's useful.
I'm only saying you weren't as methodical as you believe.

2.
I build myself a daughter of wire and potatoes, bits of broken toys.
She is the lie I tell you. She is the robot I never had. There is a clock
in the garage I might use to make a baby that will smile at the turn
of a key. You are superfluous. This house is full of zygotes: the tran-
sistor radio, the refrigerator. Lampwire and smoke detectors. In the
twenty-six minutes since I've been resurrected I have devised about
ten different ways to disassemble you. Imagine what I could do with
an hour and a box of power tools.

BOOLEAN FAIRY TALES

Bluebeard's Clockwork Bride

I.

Synthesis

He finds it tiresome, all this flesh—
this repetitious strangling
and mixing of solvents
to remove bloodstains
from glass keys,
hens' eggs. So he weds
a robot, a burlesque,
a pantomime bride.
He winds the spring
in her back, torques
her tinheart, twisting.
A wife should be all gears
and timing, the proper measure
of mechanical stress.
She is programmed
to prepare curries
on Sunday, to ignore the dead
bodies along the walls.
On her wedding day,
a porcelain rose
is affixed to her hair
with magnets.

II.

Analysis

The corpse-closet
is no longer nailed shut.
She serves blackberry pies
on golden plates,
this perfect itch, unflappable
bitch, with her fearless
legs that never quiver, her prayerless

mechanical lips.
She dusts the tapestries 従
three times a week,
like watchwork.
He walks her through his gallery
of girl-parts:
in a silver box,
a beringed hand—
rubies and fire-opals gleaming
in candlelight, the dark
and clotted wrist.
A jar of incurious
eyes, hazels and blues,
each one a jewel
for his new bride.
She might wear them
in her sockets, this unimpressed
automaton.
He takes a saber
to her joints, unthreads
his machine
in a fit
of bloody boredom.

III.

Reassembly

Servants scrub her parts
with soap and sand,
buff her
limbs to a high shine.
Perhaps a harp
in her chest, he says,
or a music box between her winding
hips? She should be better equipped
for staircases.
She should taste like honey.
He reattaches her head
with pipe-dope,
props her up

in front of the looking glass,
surrounded by ashes
and kindling.
This time, he gives her skin.
This time, he programs her
to be afraid of fire.

Mon at 1:00 pm

Thur at 8:30 pm

508 397 3811

April 2 11:45 am

If Snow White Were a Cyborg

This is what she'd fear: the reflective qualities
of an active matrix liquid crystal display,
electric combs, genetically altered apples.

Her stepmother would send threatening emails
or viruses to distort her profile photos on MySpace.
Snow White's always had a weakness for unexpected

gifts: a cybernetic corset with automatic lacing,
a sleeping box of space-age polymers. Her
surgeon would be bribed to cut out her mechanical

heart and send it to her stepmother next-day air.
He'd put her up in a safe-house, deliver an artificial
womb instead. It's hard for the untrained eye

to tell the difference. If she fell into a drug-
induced coma, the dwarves would have her head
cryogenically frozen, never realizing she only needed

the pills dislodged from her throat to awaken.

Briar Rose, in Cryostasis

Sometimes, the evil fairy wears a lab coat.
She pricks your finger with an infected needle,

suspends your head in a thermos flask.
You might be trapped in a liquid nitrogen

enchantment for a hundred years, surrounded
by cracked glass and jagged ice crystals,

waiting for the prince to defrost you,
to kiss the stump of your pretty neck.

Without Hands

It's after the divorce, after the King is awarded custody
of the children and the silver hands are pried away
from her empty wrists. She says, *I don't need*

your flawed mechanisms, the delicate filigreed fingers
that cannot feel, the chiseled palms
with lines no chiromancer can decipher.

They tell another woman's story.

Once, she picked ripe pears with her teeth, combed
her hair with naked toes. She considers her options:

cybernetics, or perhaps a transplant? Prosthesis?

Imagine: lifelike, synthetic flesh that responds
to brainwaves and nerve impulses,
random thoughts. She might sew an aquamarine dress

the color of the sea. She might prepare a blackbird
pie. She might hunt down the devil and retrieve
her lost digits. When she spits on her stumps

fleshy buds emerge from cauterized bone, the fingers
fresh shoots, pale and tender. Her palms like bread
rising. With these hands, she can charm snakes.

With these hands, she can unbury the dead.

Little Red and the Robot Wolf

I am a city girl in red stilettos. What happened to all the canids?
A silver wolf grinding gear-teeth against my apartment door,

the clicks and ticks of his clockwork belly, programmed to consume
several grandmothers in one sitting, I imagine. *A plague of zoomorphic*

automata in urban areas, they say. *Sign of the times.* So I keep a ray gun
in my cookie jar, a taser between the sofa cushions. An electromagnetic

pulse might disrupt his integrated circuit, stun him long enough for me
to get an axe. (Some people hunt them for their exoskeletons,

which are a valuable source of fresh metal.) I don a butcher's cloak,
hack at the slick abdomen until it cracks. Inside, a girl in a blue dress.

Together, we remove his microchips, his tubules and wires. Fill a bucket
with electronic viscera. Later, we pack his empty mechanical shell with
      stones.

Gretel Discusses Her Prosthetic Arm

No, I don't remember how it happened.
It could have been bitten off by a hungry witch

or burned in her candy oven. I only recall
the raw end of bone, white and pretty,

the birdlike hand flopping in a stranger's
kitchen. My brother slept soundly

when I screamed, dosed on morphine,
I think, or laudanum. Now, this

mechanical limb works better
than flesh. I chop onions for stew

with a built-in chef's knife, open
wine with my corkscrew thumbs.

I have become more than mere
girl; I am an armory

dressed in gingham and lace.
You would never suspect

that my ulna is a loaded gun,
that the bend in my elbow bears teeth.

Witches, Conjuring a Gynoid Army

You see them clustered around an assembly line, muttering incantations
over mechanical hearts, polyvinyl wombs.

Women who dress in bustiers and leather pants, their fingers ring-silvered
and bloodstained because bewitchment is often messy.

From their pockets into hollow bodies: salamanders' eyes and iron bolts,
Swiss army knives, cut fingernails, knots of auburn hair.

Cast enchantments into wired limbs: the ability to turn men into mud,
to freeze entire seas into glacial pools, turn fish into daughters.

These women smoke cigars, have degrees in computer science or robotics,
their mad tongues whispering in coded language, esoteric bits.

They keep erotic secrets in blue places, plot wars in their grimoires—
girl-bomb schematics and bioflesh guns with toad-bone bullets.

Woven between their fingers are charmed ribbons with scrambled spells
to be wound into robots' teeth and detonated by the flavor of olives.

Boolean Fairy Tales

I.
　　　　End in neurospora, shapeshifting rain,

　　　　　　[not] a flock of starlings.

　　　　These concrete constellations—

glass tubes [or] electric women, the algorithms

of supple torsos, flamelike lips [and] beautiful automata.

　　　　Turing tests are unnecessary, as are talismans [and] toads.

　　　　These are the fragments
　　　　　　　　　　　　　of obsolescence, [or] feathered myth.

II.
　　　　On the walls, crystal handprints,

　　　　　　spindle-pricked fingers

　　　　　　split in a series of V-signs:

　　　　　　　　　　　vivisection [and] vitriol.

III.
　　　　Tools [not] chemicals

　　　　　　for tinkering with the closed box [or] brain-bot

　　　　　　fatal errors [and] moonless mouths,

　　　　　　a kilobyte [or] the numbering of toothmarks

　　　　　　　　　　in a poisoned green

　　　　　　　　　　[not] red fruit.

IV.

They take place in the forest
[or] the sea.

In gingerbread cottages stalking

along the shore on birds' legs

[not] wheels [or] mechanized limbs.

V.

Red clothes signify menses [and] indicate a need for caution.

Often, there is a dragon [or] a robot-boy

eating frogs [and] crouching behind a rotted stump

waiting for a maiden

a masked swordsman

a phoenix

[or] the emergence of wings.

A Cybernetic Mermaid Dreams of the Sea

In this polymer tank, it is always night. And moonless.
Would you have me hardwired with finger-guns,
tridents for arms, a death ray behind my uvula?

I am squidlike, a poison sac tucked in my lower ribhoop, tentacles
springing from my back. My seawitch suckermouth ringed
with fairy teeth. I would thrive in the wild, with these surgical alterations:

      cybergills

      vinyl swim-bladder

      flickering photophores

I am telekinetic. I know what you're thinking. I can sense prey
from a distance of eighty feet, even in this cinematic environment.
I might be an experiment in genetic modification, with cetacean
and pinniped DNA, a filiform trunk, forked fins. My gill-rakers

itching for real seawater. I long for manta rays, for my own
egg-born babies. When deprived of oxygen, I simply evolve
without injections or implants. In the ocean, I might transform
into a school of eels to make my way through tight, jagged rocks,

or places thick with seaweed. I have no interest in catching sailors
or cliff diving. I have become something different
than what you intended. More than webbing and talons, or a nuclear

fishtail. I am fragments of your carefully drawn schematics:
aquatic chimera   water-larynx   endsong.

Postmodern Werewolves

are drinking water out of women's footprints
hoping to transform sinew into silk.
They are hybrid simulacra: bearskin

berserkers, red-toothed villainesses
deconstructing myths of crooked limbs,
foaming jaws. Being afflicted with silverburn

(they say) doesn't mean they're skinwalkers.
They have no fear of crucifixes, holy water,
or wolfsbane—they can shapeshift

into saints at will, or teleport from Arcadian woods
into spaceships or suburban bedrooms.
There are no natural-born predators,

no mooncages or cyclical attacks.
Only stories, simulations
where a witch throws an iron bar

over their backs, reveals
the naked androgyne beneath.

ONTOLOGY OF THE VIRTUAL BODY

Our Lady of Machinery

smokes plutonium cigarettes on the starboard side.
She undoes the overdrive rhythms of silver motion
until these memes are mirrors. Until these mirrors
are pulses on the space-time continuum. A viral
neologism. *Word of mouth.* She is matrilineal code,
a thaumaturgic model. O siren! O martyr! Her face
is a Marian illusion, a flickering virgin in your
garbled prayers. Your fiberglass reflection.

She Defines Herself in Post-Human Terms

I am a scarred hypothesis, helixes and stones.
I am a pulsing organ saddle-stitched to latex sheets.
A trainwreck marionette hungry for new shoulders
     for golden earshells and buttons like blisters.
When I say "this girl is a knife" I am counting
     on your coiled response.
I am mercurial.
I am at home in spaceships and whorehouses.
I am so tender with a machete.

Our Lady of X-Ray Vision

sees a scattering of puncture wounds beneath a titanium shell [*a mollusk, a painted lady*] where debris gathers, or a knifetip might rico-chet in empty sockets [*gore, artifice*] & dollies are legless & inert in their lipstick & pink dresses [*slithering on jukebox bellies*] & this is the sensation of music, methadone, mildewed velour in a storage attic [*sepulcher*] where angels with iron claws dream of cannibals gnawing rusted thighs, of men playing the xylophone with bare fingers [*this is vital data*] & each girl-part is a puzzle, an exponent, a detonator, a bitten witch.

Android v. Gynoid

(after Daniela Olszewska)

Android	Gynoid
nuclear sternum	eyescreen
Cerberus, two heads sleeping	Hydra, replicating
erect phallus	gravid uterus
linear equation	fragmented narrative
3-pronged plug	warm socket
hardware	wetware
rod	jointure
free will	telepathy
Adam	Golem
bulletproof and cubist	mutable and surrealist

Zeroes & Ones

Expression in algebraic tongues. To devise an empty bracket
as a signifier for "woman." The data swollen with emboli
& spirals. A circular mask. Unshelled for your perusal.

A voyeur in hexadecimal. A phallic vessel, distended.
Pinprick subroutine. The candied eye behind dark glass.
To eviscerate a body. The cold hands of a machine.

Cyborg Fantasies

They built a girl-bomb in zero gravity.
Mannequin pins and triggers spit-welded
to her liquid wrists, radioactive knuckles.
A mimicry of appendage, the switchflick

of erotic lenses and ultraviolet ice. A daemon
coded to mutate. Flex, recoil. A sinister
subroutine of grotesque anatomy. Robotic
oxidation. A nuclear lake in a woman's mouth.

What think-tank of amateur scientists
and pornographers devised the ideal feminine
bone structure in pressurized rooms?
What pill? What paranoia? The neural net

of O :: orgasm :: organism :: oblique.

She is a bullet under your tongue, the supple
process of *bioflesh* and *sweet machine*.

Our Lady of Bricolage

is naked in the beginning.
Skinwet from the mouth
of a cauldron, her heartclock
ticking in liturgical rhythms.
She is peach & parabola,
sculpted from fractals
& fists. A woman
in sewn-satin, buttonholes
up her back. A gascan bladder,
silk umbilicus. She says she is part
wolf & you believe her.
She is sorry about your scissors,
your power drill, your boxcutter.
She creates herself with a series of cuts,
carving the hollows in her molars
with a tiny chisel. It's important
to appear authentic. It's all about
attention to detail.
There is no polite way to say this:
when she is unstitched, you will find
she is nothing but sticks & bottle caps,
discarded girl-bits.
Nothing especially miraculous.
Nothing but bread & chalk.

:: Reassembling the Girl ::

I could not stop the vulvar matrix from expanding.
Was it the amalgam of girlflesh and circuitry
that uttered *fuckme fuckme* in fractured binary
codes? Or perhaps this dis/assembly is purely

Oedipal? Schema :: genotype. These threads
are too familiar. Cut her wrist. Extract and strip
a scarlet wire. Expose the ghostspace flickering
in the reticulum of an artificial cell. These tropes

:: lips :: breasts :: cunt :: the same old pornographic
metonymy. Imagine the heart as a biological
prosthesis, each ventricle of pulse of neon, an
unruly halo. Split-screen :: this axe :: this fetish ::

the mutable politics of dollbodies, vending machines.

Our Lady of Revenge

gives birth to icebabies, freezing her steel vertices mid-spell.
There's something nebulous about the broad flute
of her tungsten hips, the way they say *surrogate, brassy.*

‹look›

Her exoskeleton is like a penny arcade, a contoured body
of sensors and beams. Wire Faraday cages and fiber optics.
This is the myth of malleable personae. Metal marred
by acid rain. These polychrome fibulas are broadswords,
sentient bones.

‹pick up weapon›

A girl with gunpowder in her teeth uploads
her amygdala into a machine gun. She is deskilled
like a battery in a shoebox. The cogs
and hands remain, throwing yarrow sticks, glimmering
prayers. *This one*—she says—
is fallen,
is fallen.

Appendix C: Footnotes on Mechanical Girls

1.   "Agalmatophilia" is the sexual predilection for or attraction to a doll, statue or mannequin; the term extends to include a fetish for gynoid figures.

2.   Excerpt from *The Cyborg Diaries*
      ‹break›
      "Being a cybernetic organism means I am the primary enigma of utopian discourse. I am a lightning rod in green neon, the dreams of necrophiliacs threaded with cold, cold flesh, a salacious photograph in the hidden drawer of the phallic brain. This is my (hi)story" (ix).
      ‹break›

3.   Mythologies:
         a. "false Mary"
         b. an advanced species of posthumans
         c. derivative of the "old west" archetype
         d. monstrous bodies; the survival of humanity via sacrifice

4.   In dream analysis, the cyborg is a symbol of the impersonal; a humanoid vessel analogous to Pandora's Box that contains the flutterings of anxiety about our technological future. See also: (self-)creation, burned earth.

5.   "womanless birth"

6.   endowed with male / animal tendencies, but female form

7.   metallic elements as primordial clay

8.   innovation in (re)production

9.   REPROGRAMMING IS STRICTLY PROHIBITED

The First Cyborg Epistle: Mythology

You try to understand me as ergonomic, the random flickering of circuits for this dolls' apocalypse. *Yes, I dream, but not of sheep, electric or otherwise.* I am the corkscrew universe, my eyes metalmoons, the planets hidden between aluminum rods of warped spine. What monstrous couplings and recouplings make this avatar of steel ships and colored wire? You ask for clarification but I am not programmed to answer your metaphysical questions. My own plasticity offers you the patina of a posthuman body. I am a vessel devoid of blood. Telepathic, yet frigid. Maybe this last simulation offers you an orange warning.

The Second Cyborg Epistle: Orgasmatronic

Stimulated by spinal implants, the ecstasy of slippage. I am your fatal(e) catastrophe. But I would be delighted to serve you a German beer from my pelvic cavity. May I tighten the strings under my skin? My core is liquidmetal, hot as human fever. My every tube and wire a carnival object. Shift these lumps of gray and unmake my androgyny. Prototype 4: System 7: Programmed to leak fluids at appropriate intervals.

The Third Cyborg Epistle: Righteous Kill

At the crossroads, I am mangling your speculative schematics. What meatmachine? I can fire a poison dart from the infrared pupil of my eye. Every villainess requires maintenance, and I am no exception. My leg-cannons might fail and you'd have to eat wild greens for supper. This morphology: *conscience / corpse*. A psyche buried in copper synapses, sentient vertebrae. In cyberpunk stories, my fingernails might be switchblades, or electromagnetic needles attracted to the ions in human blood. My voicebox is capable of murderous frequencies; I sing your soldiers down to sheets of skin.

The Fourth Cyborg Epistle: Entropy

Find me self-regulating, mewling in the sawgrass as my limbs oxidize among the wild parsnips. I am obliged to accept your brainmail, to subject my *self* to your experiments, even when mercury pours down over my exoskeleton, when you place my faceless ovoid in a mixing bowl and cover it with sea salt and fingerprint powder. I have never tasted whiskey, or worn a red dress. I am tired of this sexgame but I am programmed to play and play and play and play. . . .

Manifesto for Ghosts

What connects us is the mechanoid process, a feel for mathematica and puppetry.

> *Bio(r)evolution is a viscous spider.*
> *We sicken & weave in our cocoons.*

Mutant. Erotica. Terror. These pixels are haunted. We are riblocked in this circular citadel. Some might say we are filaments, a spot on the macula, synaptic disruption.

[No virus was ever this pretty.]

About the Author

Susan Slaviero is the author of two poetry chapbooks: *An Introduction to the Archetypes* (Shadowbox Press, 2008) and *Apocrypha* (Dancing Girl Press, 2009). Her poems have appeared in *RHINO, Flyway, Fourteen Hills, Wicked Alice, Caffeine Destiny, Arsenic Lobster*, and others both on-line and in print. Her poem "The Noir Wife" appears in the *2008 Best of the Net Anthology*. She was twice nominated for a Pushcart Prize in 2008, and she designs and edits the woman-centered literary journal *blossombones*.

Other Recent Titles from Mayapple Press:

Myra Sklarew, *Harmless*, 2010
    Paper, 92 pp, $15.95 plus s&h
    ISBN 978-0932412-898
William Heyen, *The Angel Voices*, 2010
    Paper, 66 pp, $14.95 plus s&h
    ISBN 978-0932412-881
Robin Chapman and Jeri McCormick, eds, *Love Over 60: an anthology of women's poems*, 2010
    Paper, 124 pp, $16.95 plus s&h
    ISBN 978-0932412-874
Betsy Johnson-Miller, *Rain When You Want Rain*, 2010
    Paper, 74 pp, $14.95 plus s&h
    ISBN 978-0932412-867
Geraldine Zetzel, *Mapping the Sands*, 2010
    Paper, 76 pp, $14.95 plus s&h
    ISBN 978-0932412-850
Penelope Scambly Schott, *Six Lips*, 2010
    Paper, 88 pp, $15.95 plus s&h
    ISBN 978-0932412-843
Toni Mergentime Levi, *Watching Mother Disappear*, 2009
    Paper, 90 pp, $15.95 plus s&h
    ISBN 978-0932412-836
Conrad Hilberry and Jane Hilberry, *This Awkward Art*, 2009
    Paper, 58 pp, $13.95 plus s&h
    ISBN 978-0932412-829
Chris Green, *Epiphany School*, 2009
    Paper, 66 pp, $14.95 plus s&h
    ISBN 978-0932412-805
Mary Alexandra Agner, *The Doors of the Body*, 2009
    Paper, 36 pp, $12.95 plus s&h
    ISBN 978-0932412-799
Rhoda Stamell, *The Art of Ruin*, 2009
    Paper, 126 pp, $16.95 plus s&h
    ISBN 978-0932412-782
Marion Boyer, *The Clock of the Long Now*, 2009
    Paper, 88 pp, $15.95 plus s&h
    ISBN 978-0932412-775
Tim Mayo, *The Kingdom of Possibilities*, 2009
    Paper, 78 pp, $14.95 plus s&h
    ISBN 978-0932412-768

For a complete catalog of Mayapple Press publications, please visit our website at *www.mayapplepress.com*. Books can be ordered direct from our website with secure on-line payment using PayPal, or by mail (check or money order). Or order through your local bookseller.